Walk & Pray

Exercise your Body and Exercise Your Faith
Confessions and Meditations

Lisa B. Taylor

DEDICATION

This book is dedicated to World Transformers. To people who understand that they can make a difference, who believe that they can make an impact, who are willing to take a risk and do something about the circumstances of their lives, families, communities, and nations, and who want to transform the world in which they live.

Tamiko Jackson, Maxine McCluney, and Diane Sublett, you are the World Transformers who believed in the vision, took the risk, and helped pioneer the *Walk & Pray*. I am forever grateful to each of you. May God truly bless you!

CONTENTS

Introduction   i

Beginnings   1

Our Beginning   5

Your Beginning   9

Scriptures: Pray, Confess, and Meditate   13

     Walking   15

     Prayer   23

     Your Position in Christ   27

     Family   33

     Husband/Father   35

     Wife/Mother   39

     Children   43

     The Church/The Body of Christ   47

     The Community   51

     The Government   55

     Blessings and Prosperity   57

Prayer Journal   63

Chart Your Walk   99

Notes   121

Get Started: Expand Your World Impact!   127

INTRODUCTION

~ *You can change your world.* ~

This book was written with a two-fold purpose in mind. First, it is designed for people who want to impact the world in which they live. You may have prayed and talked to God concerning your situation and/or crisis. You may have cried or complained about the things that concern you within your family, neighborhood, city, state, country, or world. Well, this book is a solution to your dilemma. No longer do you have to feel hopeless or helpless. You have the power to impact and bring transformation in the areas that concern you. The most effective ways that you can bring about change is through prayer and by taking action.

Oftentimes, people find things that they can complain about, but rarely do they pray about those things. I believe that a person should not complain about anything that he or she is not willing to pray about and/or do something about in order to make a change.

Second, not only do we need to pray and take action, but we also need to take care of our bodies—the vehicles that transport us everywhere we go. The body is the temple of the Holy Spirit and so many of us do not maintain our temples properly. With heart disease, diabetes, strokes, cancers, obesity, back injuries, arthritis, anxiety, depression, etc., just to name a few, being major health problems for people these days, it is obvious that it is time to stop complaining and start doing something. As it relates to matters of the heart, it is time to get heart healthy. Out of the heart flow the issues of life.[1] Moreover, as it relates to so many aliments that people are facing, it is not just about what we are eating, but what is eating us. Having said that, it is time to let God perfect those things that concern us and maintain our cause.[2] However, faith without works is dead.[3] We need wisdom on how to maintain our bodies.

Therefore, in order to create change in our situations, we must become proactive. We must get about doing those things that create well-being and give us life and vitality. Moreover, we must learn to let our actions say "no" to the things that are detrimental to our health and well-being, our families and communities, and the world in which we live. Furthermore, we must begin to say "yes" to the things that bring us wholeness and life, peace and prosperity, and purpose and meaning.

It is high time for the common man and woman to stand up and be counted. Why wait for others to make change when you have it within your power to do so? You have the power and ability to effect change and be a part of history? You can make a difference in the world that you live in. You can impact the society that your children and grandchildren will live in. Moreover, you can be a positive influence in every area of life that concerns you. You don't have to sit passively by waiting for somebody else to do something about the situation. You are the somebody. Look in the mirror and say, "I am the Somebody who can do

---

[1] Proverbs 4:24.
[2] Psalms 138:8; 140:12.
[3] James 2:26b.

something about (state whatever it is that you want to do something about or see changed)!" You are the one who can revolutionize the world in which you live.

As you get ready to make an impact and create change in the areas that concern you, be mindful that change does not come without a fight. Whenever you set yourself to stand up against anything or to make a change, even if it is something as simple as losing a couple of pounds, a battle takes place. You say, "I'm not going to eat sweets." It seems like, as soon as you utter the words, all you want to do is eat sweets. The same thing happens when you decide to make changes in other areas of your life. In order to bring about change, you must be ready, willing, and able to stand and fight for it. You must be willing to do what it takes. If necessary, you must be willing to take it. According to Scripture, even when the kingdom of heaven suffers violence, the violent take it by force.[4]

In my opinion, most Christians are willing to sit by idly and take whatever the devil or society throws at them. In fact, some of them are not willing to stand up for anything. I do not know about you, but I refuse to be counted among those who had the power, ability, and authority[5] to effect change and did nothing. I believe that if a man is not willing to stand or die for something, then he is not willing to live for anything. It is time for the Body of Christ to take a stand. It is time for us to make a difference in the world in which we live. It is time for Christians to take the challenge and say, "Yes, I will make the difference and transform the world in my generation." If you are a

---

[4] Matthew 11:12

[5] According to Matthew 28:18-20, Jesus Christ has been given all power and authority. He told us to go into every man's world and make disciples and He ensures us that He is with us.

world transformer, then *Walk & Pray* is for you. You and the generations to come will benefit greatly from *Walk & Pray*. You will take action and transform the world that you live in, as you exercise your body and exercise your faith consecutively.

Before you begin to *Walk & Pray*, it is important to understand that prayer is simply communication with God. When you pray, you just talk to God about the things that concern you. Moreover, prayer has a purpose. The purpose of prayer is effective two-way communication. First, prayer is you talking to God and God talking back to you. Second, prayer is God listening to you and you listening to God. This two-way communication is important to discovering the mind, heart, will, and plans of God, so that you will be able to pray and get results.

Prayer is so powerful and impactful that it is the only thing that Jesus' disciples asked him to teach them how to do.[6] When they asked, he gave them an outline for prayer that has been entitled, "The Lord's Prayer." Moreover, he gave them a scenario that demonstrated the power of asking and receiving from God.[7] Additionally, Jesus taught about prayer in His Sermon on the Mount, where He contrasted how the religious leaders prayed to draw attention to themselves with how a person should pray to gets results.[8] To get results in prayer, a person should enter his/her closet, shut the door, and pray to his/her Father in secret, then his/her Father, who sees in secret will reward him/her openly.

In order to know what Jesus is really saying to his

---

[6] Luke 11:1-4.
[7] Luke 11:5-13.
[8] Matthew 6:5-13.

followers, it is important that you understand the Biblical Greek meaning for the words *closet*, *secret*, and *openly*. The Greek word for *closet* is *tameion*, which means a "storage chamber," "storeroom," "chamber especially an inner chamber," and/or a "secret room."[9] This word derives from the word that means dispenser or distributor. The Greek word for *secret* is *kryptos*, which means hidden or concealed.[10] The Greek word for *openly* is *phaneros*, which means apparent, manifest, evident, known, and to be plainly recognized or known.[11] When we look at the meaning of these three words, it is easy to see what Jesus was saying. In my own paraphrase, Jesus was saying, "When you pray, you should enter into your storeroom, inner chamber, secret room, or distribution center and ask God in a manner that is not known, and God will reward you in a way that is apparent and evident. He will make it known."

When I first discovered the meaning of these three words, I got excited because I realized that Jesus was instructing me to pray to God in a manner where I went into my storeroom, secret room, and/or distribution center, the place where I meet with God, the place where everything that I need is already present and God would make it known that I had been there. My prayer life would be evident and made known by the manifestation of the answers to my prayers. Why? Because God would meet me there, hear me there, answer me there, and then manifest the answer to my prayers.

Another critical key to prayer is found in Matthew 6:8,

---

[9] Strong, J., "tameion," (Strong's G5009), Strong's Exhaustive Concordance of the Bible (Logos Electronic Scholar's Library, 2015).
[10] Strongs., J. "kryptos," (Strong's G2927).
[11] Strong, J., "phaneros," (Strong's G5318).

where Jesus says that the Father knows what you have need of before you ask. However, Jesus instructs us to ask. Even though God is a mind reader, a heart regulator, a planner who has finished the works before the foundation of time, we must ask. We must ask, seek, and knock, so that we can receive, find, and have the door opened to us. You are not responsible for answering our own prayers, God is. However, you are responsible for praying, for asking, for having two-way conversations with God. If you ask, you will receive.

Additionally, prayer is to be consistent and constant. Jesus tells his followers a parable about a widow who continued to ask an unjust judge to vindicate her.[12] The moral of this story is that we should always pray and not faint. The Apostle Paul helps us understand this concept of consistent and constant prayer by telling us to "pray without ceasing."[13] Finally, when we pray, we should find out what God's Word says about the situation, circumstance, or concern. The Bible says that God is watching over His Word to perform it.[14] It also says that the Word of God is not void of power. It will not return to God empty, but it shall accomplish God's purpose and succeed in the thing for which He sent it.[15] What better way to do that than to have an ongoing conversation and/or dialogue with God? As you learn to pray and get results, you will realize prayer is an investment and it comes with benefits.

You do not have to wait for blessings and benefits to fall out of the sky one day. You do not have to sit around wishing, hoping, and begging for blessings and benefits.

---

[12] Luke 18:1-8.

[13] 1 Thessalonians 5:17.

[14] Jeremiah 1:12.

[15] Isaiah 55:11.

Your blessings and benefits are closer than you might think or imagine. Not only are they very near, but they are also consistent. God daily loads you with benefits.[16] I believe that walking and praying are among the many benefits that God daily loads you with. He gives you the ability to walk and pray. It doesn't matter if you can walk fast or walk slow. The only thing that matters is that you start. Here are a few of the benefits of walking and prayer:

Benefits of Walking

- Burns almost as many calories as jogging
- Eases back pains
- Slims your waist
- Lowers blood pressure
- Reduces levels of bad cholesterol
- Reduces heart attack risk
- Enhances stamina and energy
- Lessens anxiety and tension
- Reduces stress
- Improves muscle tone
- Reduces appetite
- Slows down osteoporosis bone loss

Benefits of Prayer

- Provides a vehicle to communicate with God
- Builds confidence
- Strengthens faith
- Eliminates anxiety and its affects
- Changes things and brings about transformation
- Brings answers and solutions
- Brings assurance and reassurance

---

[16] Psalms 68:19; 103:2.

- Brings deliverance, salvation, healing, restoration, etc.
- Produces instructions, strategies, tactics, etc.
- Provides mercy and help

These lists are not intended to be exhaustive. However, they have been provided as a motivator to get you walking and praying. They have also been provided to help you understand the purpose of the *Walk & Pray*. You may still be asking, "Why walk and pray?" Well, let me explain. The purpose of the Walk & Pray is to encourage well-being[17] as we engage and transform the communities in which we live through the power of prayer and corporate efforts as we pray for our children, families, communities, churches, governments, officials, and nations.

Furthermore, as you look at your health, family, community, church, and world in which you live, you may have constantly cried, "Is there not a cause?" Know for certain that there is a cause and you are the answer. You can effect change. You have the power to transform the world that you live in. You have the power to make a difference.

In order to assist you with your *Walk & Pray*, this book is composed of tools to equip you. Within this book, you will find scriptures that you can confess, meditate on, and pray. These scriptures are designed as a tool to help impact and transform you and the things that concern you. For the purpose of this book, be mindful that the word meditation does not mean to keep silent. It refers to the words "to mutter." You are to speak the words to yourself. Moreover, everyday you are to confess aloud the promises of God's Word in this book to yourself and corporately

---

[17] 1 Timothy 2:1-4.

with others. Confess and pray God's Word over the things that concern you. As you confess and pray the promises of God's Word, they will transform you and the areas in which you speak His Word. In this book, the promises of God have been personalized for you and they address some of the areas that may concern you.

Just as Adam heard the voice of God when he was walking in the garden in the cool of the day, so can you. As you walk, God can speak to you and give you divine instructions. He can instruct you in the way that you should go. He will give you His desires, so that you can pray them. Walking and praying may seem foolish, but it is a simple strategy that the common man, woman, and child can utilize to impact the world in which they live. All you have to do is *begin*.

BEGINNINGS

When God gives a vision, He always gives provision. To the one who has been assigned to obey the voice of God, the provision may seem small. When the provisions arrive, you may even second-guess yourself. You know what God showed you and it looks nothing like the provisions that are at hand. You may even say to yourself, "God, I know what you showed me and I can't get anything done with this skimpy little stuff that I have now."

Since you are the one who captures the vision and begins to contemplate, ponder, talk about, and even cry over the vision, you may deny what you have seen if you only look at what *appears* to be the provisions. You saw the greatness of the vision and you know what God said. However, when you prayed for God to show you what to do and how to do it, the next steps may have been blurry. When you look at the vision, the provisions, purpose, and destiny, you heart becomes overwhelmed.

You know what you saw. You know what you heard. You know what you must do, but the provisions are small.

At this point, some people would give up. They would deny the God given desire of their heart and go to their graves never fulfilling their life's call – never fulfilling their purpose. Think about it! As human being, whether Christian or not, we are quick to think about what we can't do because of. As Christians, we often forget that we are not alone in our endeavors. The One who has promised is faithful,[18] but we can be faithless.

In a day and time, where we measure our success by who we are and what we do, even as Christians, we fall short. We fall short, disobey God, and give up quickly because we don't understand beginnings. According to Merriam-Webster, the word "beginning" is a verb which means "to do the first part of an action: go into the first part of process: START."[19]

With this in mind, we must understand that when God gives us a vision for our lives, our families, our businesses, our careers, our ministries, our communities, our nations, etc., He reveals the end from the beginning. Therefore, the vision that is revealed is an already finished work. God shows us the completion of His vision and/or work. At first sight, we do one of two things. First, we rejoice in the fact that God would use us. Second, we become overwhelmed with the vision and how it is going to come to pass. We begin to contemplate, "How can I do it? How can I obey God and complete the vision that he has shown me?"

Again, we forget that He who has promised is faithful.[20]

---

[18] Deuteronomy 7:9; 1 Thessalonians 5:24; Hebrews 10:23.
[19] Beginning. (n.d.). Retrieved January 15, 2016, from http://www.merriam-webster.com/dictionary/beginning.p;

We also forget that the vision is a complete work and our only responsibility is to trust God. At this moment, we must exercise our faith. True faith is evidenced by works, by action. The Apostle James said that faith without works is dead.[21] Therefore, if we would only exercise our faith and *begin*, we would see the salvation of the Lord. We would see the manifestation of His promises. We would see God's purpose and will manifested in the areas of vision that He has shown us. We would become world transformers and effect change in the areas that God is showing us to concentrate our efforts.

Remember where there is vision, there is also provisions. We must exercise our faith and not despise small beginnings.

---

[20] Hebrews 10:23.
[21] James 2:26b.

OUR BEGINNING

~ Nothing is too difficult if you just start. ~

Beginning the *Walk & Pray* did not come without challenges. When God first gave me the vision, I was excited. However, the excitement as short lived. By the time I finished thinking about the awesome task ahead, my mind was loaded down with questions, concerns, failures, successes, etc.… I had magnified everything that could go wrong, while minimizing the things that could go well. I knew that I heard God's voice and the desire of His heart. However, my heart grew faint, as I wondered who would get involved.

In some Christian arenas, people only get involved if their organization initiates or endorses the program, service, or movement. Even though I was aware of this obstacle, I could not let it deter me from obeying God. Therefore, I just continued to share the vision with people within my circle of family, friends, and acquaintances. On the day that the *Walk & Pray* began, only those who believed that it was time for a change showed up. We began with four world transformers—that is three ladies and me.

We showed up at a local park and walked from 6:00 a.m. until 6:45 a.m. After walking for 45 minutes, we would pray, and then the ladies would leave the park at 7:00 a.m. headed for work. God gave us strategy for each day. We began walking from Monday thru Friday, but the ladies insisted that we add Saturday and Sunday. Since God had given us detailed strategy, we had to include these two days too. I was amazed by the ladies' willingness, excitement, and commitment.

Here I was wondering who would join me in the park so early in the morning and God sent a group of women who captured the vision and ran with it. Throughout our times in the park, these ladies encouraged me, gave me hope, and strengthened my faith. They dreamed and prayed with me about the future of the *Walk & Pray* and we experienced the hand of God at work.

Some days just seeing the ladies get out of their cars motivated me to move forward with the vision. I believe the motivation and excitement continued, as we were able to pray for and with people who were just wandering around in the park at 6:00 a.m. in the morning. You would be amazed, but God isn't. He gave us an opportunity to pray for and bless so may people.

I remember one gentleman who saw us huddled together. He came over to ask us for a light. We didn't have the kind of light he was looking for, but we were able to tell him about the Light of the World, Jesus Christ. We also told him about our congregating to *Walk & Pray* every morning. When he heard about the prayer, he asked us to pray for him and his girlfriend. On another occasion, one of the ladies' mother was diagnosed with cancer. We took this assault personally and we began to pray. I am happy to share with you that God heard and answered our prayer. During this time, He also strengthened our faith. Not only that, but we began to see things happening in the communities that we prayed for. To this day, we believe that we ignited the hearts of the leadership in our city to call for prayer like never before.

Today we continue to believe God for the *Walk & Pray*. By faith, we thank God for all the people who are now involved in the simple strategy that God gave us. We believe more people will get involved and become world transformers. We envision a world where God's will is manifesting as people just simply *Walk & Pray*.

If this book is in your hand, then you didn't just pick it up by chance. You are a world transformer. You are one of the people that we believed for and envisioned that God would use to manifest His will as you *Walk & Pray*. You made a decision that something needed to happen. You didn't despise small beginnings. You heard the cry for change and you took action. As you *Walk & Pray*, confessing the Word of God, the Lord will hear and answer you. May God bless your obedient endeavors!

YOUR BEGINNING

~ It's your choice, so make the best one. ~

You may be wondering, "How do I get started?" Well, you could take a few different approaches, but let me share two approaches. First, you could take the *individual approach*, meaning you could *Walk & Pray* alone. You would identify your walking location (e.g. neighborhood, parking lot, gym, track and field, trail, etc.), then you would set dates and times to walk. For instance, you might walk 3 days a week at 6 a.m. in the morning or at 6 p.m. in the evening at the park. You might decide to pray silently as you walk or you might walk, then pray after you complete your walk.

Second, you could take the *corporate approach*,[22] meaning you could *Walk & Pray* with others. You could create a *Walk & Pray* team. You and/or your team could determine the days and times that you would walk. You could also determine if you will pray as you walk or pray afterwards. Even if you and your team members choose to pray silently as you walk, you could join hands after your

---

[22] The corporate approach is a group/team method.

walk and then pray together. You could also determine what area/topic you would *Walk & Pray* about each day. This is a wonderful way to get to know the needs of each member and to pray for each other's needs. It also gives you an avenue to utilize the power of agreement in prayer, as you gather together in God's name and get Him in the midst of you.[23]

Whatever approach you take is up to you. However, I preferred the corporate approach. It gave my *Walk & Pray* team a chance to not only *exercise our bodies and exercise our faith* individually, but collectively. Another benefit of this group activity is that if anything happened, we knew that we were not in it alone. We had a support group of praying women who would pray and stand in faith with us without gossiping about us. It also gave us an opportunity to be the Lord's witness in the park where we prayed. People would see us walking, stretching, standing, and/or sitting down, and come over and ask questions about what we were doing in the park. Sometimes they might have a need. All of these opportunities were open doors to share the Gospel.

In addition, the scriptural confessions and meditations can be used as you pray for the various topics in each chapter. As you continuously make the confessions and meditate on these scriptures, you will be able to easily recall them and add them to your spontaneous or rehearsed prayers. Also, your faith will be strengthened because you will no longer wonder what or how to pray about these particular subjects. You will have the word of God about each topic at your fingertips and you can just pray it.

Be mindful that these confessions and meditations are not a "name it and claim it" formula. However, they are

---

[23] Matt. 18:19-20

faith builders that you can use as you exercise your faith, confess the promises of God, and learn how to pray the Word of God. Also, be mindful that the "Blessings and Prosperity" chapter is not only just about material riches and gain. I truly believe that God wants to bless and prosper his people, but my questions are, "Who determines what a blessing is and what is true prosperity?" From my understanding, biblical prosperity is about having everything that you need for the journey that God has purposed for your life. Believe Me! God does richly provide. He does greatly reward and prosper His people.

Therefore, this compilation of scriptural confessions and meditations is intended to help you understand who God is and what He has done, who Christ is and what He has done, and who you are and how you can live as a Word-sufficient person, living by the power of God. This is the true blessing that we have in God. The Apostle Peter said it best,

> "His [God's] divine power has granted to us all things that pertain to life and godliness, through the knowledge of him who called us to his own glory and excellence, by which he has granted us his precious and very great promises, so that through them you may become partakers of the divine nature, having escaped from the corruption that is in the world because of sinful desire. For this very reason, make every effort to supplement your faith with virtue, and virtue with knowledge, and knowledge with self-control, and self-control with steadfastness, and steadfastness with godliness, and godliness with brotherly affection, and brotherly affection with love. For if these qualities are yours and are increasing, they keep you from being ineffective or unfruitful in the

knowledge of our Lord Jesus Christ."[24]

As you *Walk & Pray*, confessing the Word of God, and praying, understand that God has, is, and will equip and empower to make a difference in the arenas of life that concern you. He has and will give you what you need, when you need it. As you *Walk & Pray*, the Lord will hear and answer you. Moreover, know for certain that when you decided to *Walk & Pray*, you made an excellent choice. May God greatly bless your labor of love!

---

[24] 2 Peter 1:3-8 (ESV).

SCRIPTURES

PRAY, CONFESS, AND MEDITATE

May you keep these scriptures in your mouth and meditate on them day and night, so that you may be careful to do according to all that is written in them. For then you will make your way prosperous, and then you will have good success. – Cross Reference Joshua 1:8

For your edification and transformation, all of these confessions and meditations have been developed from Scripture. All I know is that the Word of God works and it is not void of power. It produces what is needed, when it is needed, where it is needed, how it is needed, and to whomever it is needed. When the Word of God goes out of God's mouth, it shall not return to Him empty, but it shall accomplish His purpose and succeed in the thing that He sent it.[25] Moreover, the Word of God is alive and active, sharper than a two-edged sword and it will do what it is supposed to do in people's thoughts, hearts, and intentions.[26] Furthermore, the Word of God is God breathed and profitable for teaching, for reproof, for correction, and for training in righteousness.[27] As you confess, meditate on, and pray God's Word, your life, your family, your church, your community, and your government will be transformed by the Word and power of God.

You will notice that the confessions and meditations have scriptural references. When the reference is not the King James Version of the Bible, you will see a Bible abbreviation. For your information, I have listed them here.

Bible Versions:

AMP	The Amplified Bible
CEV	Contemporary English Version
ESV	English Standard Version
KJV	King James Version
TLB	Living Bible
MSG	The Message
NIV	New International Version
NKJV	New King James Version
NLT	New Living Translation

---

[25] Isaiah 55:11

[26] Hebrews 4:12

[27] 2 Timothy 3:16.

WALKING

1. I take a walk in every direction and explore the new possessions the Lord is giving me. ~Gen. 13:17 NLT

2. I shall follow God's rules and keep His statues and walk in them. He is the Lord my God. I shall therefore keep His statues and His rules; which if I do them, I will live by them: He is the Lord. ~Lev. 18:4-5 ESV

3. I walk in God's statues and I observe His commandments and do them, then God gives me my rains in my season, and the land shall yield its increase, and the trees of the field shall yield her fruit. My threshing shall last to the time of the grape harvest, and the grape harvest shall last to the time of sowing. And I shall eat my bread to the full and dwell in my land securely. God will give peace in the land, and I shall lie down, and none shall make me afraid. And God will remove harmful beasts from the land, and the sword shall not go through my land. I shall chase my enemies, and they shall fall before me by the sword. Five of us shall chase a hundred, and a hundred of us shall chase ten thousand, and our enemies shall fall before us by the sword. God will turn to me and make me fruitful and multiply me and He will confirm His covenant with me. I shall eat old store long kept, and I shall clear out

the old to make way for the new. God will make His dwelling among us, and His soul shall not abhor us. And He will walk among us and He will be our God and we shall be His people. ~Lev. 26:3-12 ESV

4. I shall walk in all the ways that the Lord, my God, has commanded me, that I may live, and that it may be well with me, and that I may live long in the land that I shall possess. ~Deut. 5:33 ESV

5. I shall keep the commandments of the Lord, my God, to walk [that is, to live each and every day] in His ways and fear [and worship] Him [with awe-filled reverence and profound respect]. For the Lord my God is bringing me into a good land, a land of brooks of water, of fountains and springs, flowing forth in valleys and hills; a land of wheat and barley, and vines and fig trees and pomegranates, a land of olive oil and honey; a land where I will eat bread without shortage, in which I will lack nothing; a land whose stones are iron, and out of whose hills I can dig copper. When I have eaten and am satisfied, then I shall bless the Lord my God for the good land, which He has given me. ~Deut. 8:6-10 AMP

6. The Lord, my God, requires me to *and I do joyfully* fear Him, walk in His ways, love Him, serve Him, with all my heart and with all my soul, and to keep His commandments and statues, which He commands me to do for my good. ~Deut. 10:12-13 (Note: Italics are my addition.)

7. The Lord, my God, has commanded me this day to love Him, to walk in His ways, and to keep His commandments, statues, and judgments, that I may live and multiply: and the Lord my God shall bless me in the land where I go to possess it. ~Deut. 30:16

8. Even when I walk through the valley of the shadow of death, I will fear no evil: for the Lord my God is with me. His rod and His staff comfort me. ~Ps. 23:4

9. I walk in integrity: Lord, redeem me and be merciful unto me. I have taken a stand and I will publicly praise the Lord. ~Ps. 26:11-12 KJV & NLT

10. The Lord has saved me from death and my feet from slipping, so that I can walk before Him in the land of the living. ~Ps. 56:13 TLB

11. The Lord God is a sun and shield: the Lord will give grace and glory: no good thing will He withhold from me for I walk uprightly. ~Ps. 84:11

12. Teach me your way, O Lord. I will walk in your truth. ~Ps. 86:11a

13. I am blessed because I know the passwords of praise. I walk in the light of the Lord's presence. ~Ps. 89:15 MSG & KJV

14. I behave myself wisely in a perfect way…. I will walk within my house with a perfect heart. ~Ps. 101:2

15. I walk before the Lord in the land of the living. ~Ps. 116:9

16. I walk at liberty: for I seek the precepts of the Lord. ~Ps. 119:45

17. Though I walk in the midst of trouble, you preserve my life; you stretch out your hand against the wrath of my enemies. The Lord will fulfill His purpose for me; your steadfast love, O Lord, endures forever. ~Ps. 138:7-8a

ESV

18. The Lord causes me to hear His loving kindness in the morning; for in Him I do trust. He causes me to know the way wherein I should walk; for I lift up my soul unto Him. ~Ps. 143:8

19. I am the righteousness of God by one Christ Jesus. Therefore, the Lord lays up sound wisdom for me. The Lord is my buckler for I walk uprightly. ~Prov. 2:7

20. Wisdom enters my heart and knowledge is pleasant to my soul. Discretion preserves me and understanding keeps me. Therefore, I am delivered from the evil man and the strange woman, so that I may walk in the way of good men/*women* and keep the paths of life. ~Prov. 2:10-12a, 16, & 20 (Note: Italics are my addition.)

21. I do not lose sight of the Word of the God. I keep sound wisdom and discretion and they are life for my soul and adornment for my neck. Then I will walk in your way securely and my foot will not stumble. ~Prov. 3:21-23 ESV

22. I walk in the light of the Lord. ~Isa 2:5

23. I wait upon the Lord and my strength is renewed. I mount up on wings as eagles. I run and I am not weary. I walk and not faint. ~Isa. 40:31

24. God puts His Spirit within me and causes me to walk in His statues. I keep His judgments and do them. ~Ezek. 36:27

25. According to the requirements of the Lord, I do justly, love mercy, and walk humbly with my God. ~Mic. 6:8

26. The Lord God is my strength. He makes my feet like hinds' feet. He makes me walk upon mine high places.... ~Hab. 3:19

27. Jesus Christ is the light of the world. I follow Him. Therefore, I shall not walk in darkness, but I have the light of life. ~John 8:12

28. I walk in the day. Therefore, I do not stumble because I see the light of this world. ~John 11:9

29. I walk while I have the light, so darkness will not overtake me. While I have the light, I believe in the light, so that I may become a son/*child* of light. ~John 12:35-36 NAS (Note: Italics are my addition.)

30. I was baptized into Jesus Christ; thereby, being baptized into His death. Therefore, I am buried with Him by baptism into death: that like as Christ was raised up from the dead by the glory of the Father, even so I also should walk in newness of life. ~Rom. 6:3-4

31. There is no condemnation for me because I am in Christ Jesus and I walk not after the flesh, but after the Spirit. For the law of the Spirit of life in Christ Jesus has made me free from the law of sin and death. ~Rom. 8:1-2

32. I walk properly as in the daytime, not in orgies and drunkenness, not in sexual immorality and sensuality, not in quarreling and jealousy. I put on the Lord Jesus Christ, and make no provisions to the flesh, to gratify its desires. ~Rom. 13:13-14 ESV

33. I walk by faith, not by sight. ~2 Cor. 5:7

34. For though I walk in the flesh, I do not war after the

flesh. For the weapons of my warfare are not carnal, but mighty through God to the pulling down of strongholds. The mighty weapons of my warfare cast down imaginations and every high thing that exalts itself against the knowledge of God. They bring into captivity every thought to the obedience of Christ and are always ready to revenge all disobedience, when my obedience is fulfilled. ~2 Cor. 10:3-6

35. I walk in the Spirit and I shall not fulfill the lust of the flesh. ~Gal. 5:16

36. I live in the Spirit. Therefore, I also walk in the Spirit. ~Gal. 5:25

37. I am God's workmanship, created in Christ Jesus unto good works, which God prepared beforehand, that I should walk in them. ~Eph. 2:10 ESV

38. I walk in a manner worthy of the calling I am called, with all humility and gentleness, with patience, bearing with one an love, eager to maintain the unity of the Spirit in the bond of peace. ~Eph. 4:1-3 ESV

39. I am a follower of God, as a dear child, and I walk in love, as Christ also has loved me, and has given Himself for me, and offering and sacrifice to God for a sweet smelling savor. ~Eph. 5:1-2

40. I am now light in the Lord. Therefore, I walk as a child of light (for the fruit of the Spirit is in all goodness and righteousness and truth); proving what is acceptable unto the Lord. ~Eph. 5:8-10

41. I walk circumspectly, as the wise, redeeming the time, understanding what the will of the Lord is and being

filled with the Spirit. ~Eph. 5:5-18

42. I walk worthy of the Lord unto all pleasing, being fruitful in every good work, and increasing in the knowledge of God; strengthened with all might, according to God's glorious power, unto all patience and longsuffering with joyfulness; giving thanks unto the Father, who has qualified me to share in the inheritance of the saints in the kingdom of light. ~Col. 1:10-13 KJV & NIV

43. As I have received Christ Jesus the Lord, I walk in Him. I am rooted and built up in Him, and established in the faith, as I have been taught, abounding in it with thanksgiving. ~Col. 2:6-7

44. I walk in wisdom toward those who are not Christian and I make the most of every opportunity. My speech is gracious and effective so that I will have the right answer and know how I should answer everyone. ~Col. 4:5-6 KJV & NLT

45. I walk worthy of God, who has called me unto His kingdom and glory. ~1 Thess. 2:12

46. As I have received how I ought to walk and to please God, I abound in it more and more. ~1 Thess. 4:1

47. I study to be quiet, to do my own business and to work with my own hands that I may walk honestly toward them that are not Christian and that I may lack nothing. ~1 Thess. 4:11-12 KJV & TLB

48. I walk in the light, as God is in the light. I have fellowship with all those who are in Christ and the blood of Jesus Christ, God's Son, cleanses us from all

sin. ~1 John 1:7

49. I say that I abide in Christ. Therefore, I walk in the same way in which He walked. ~1 John 2:6 ESV

50. Jesus Christ has commanded that I love. Therefore, I walk after His commandments, which I have heard from the beginning. ~John 13:34; 2 John 6

PRAYER

1. The Lord gives ear to my words. He considers my meditation. My King and my God listens to the voice of my cry for unto Him will I pray. In the morning, the Lord shall hear my voice. In the morning, I will direct my prayer to the Lord and I will look up. ~Ps. 5:1-3

2. As for me, I will call upon God; and the Lord shall save me. Evening, morning, and noon, I will pray and cry aloud and He shall hear my voice. ~Ps. 55:16-17

3. I love my enemies, bless those who curse me, do good to those who hate me, and pray for those, which despitefully use me and persecute me. ~Matt. 5:44

4. When I pray, I enter into my closet, and when I have shut my door, I pray to my Father which is in secret; and my Father which sees in secret shall reward me openly. ~Matt. 6:6

5. I watch and pray that I may not enter into temptation. ~Matt. 26:41a

6. What things I desire when I pray, I believe that I

receive them and I shall have them. ~Mark 11:24

7. Whenever I stand praying, I forgive, if I have anything against anyone, so that my Father also who is in heaven may forgive me of my trespasses. ~Mark 11:25 ESV

8. I always pray and I do not give up. ~Luke 18:1 NIV (Note: You can interchange "faint" [KJV] or "lose heart" [ESV] with "give up").

9. Whatsoever I shall ask in the name of Jesus, He will do it, so that the Father may be glorified in the Son. If I ask anything in Jesus name, He will do it. ~John 14:13-14

10. *Since* I abide in Christ and His words abide in me, I ask whatever I wish and it will be done for me. ~John 15:7 ESV (Note: Italics are my addition.)

11. This is the confidence that I have in Him, that if I ask anything according to His will (*that is consistent with His plan and purpose*) He hears me. ~1 John 5:14 KJV & AMP (Note: Italics are from the AMP.)

12. The Spirit helps me in my weaknesses. For I do not know what to pray for as I ought, but the Spirit himself intercedes for me with groanings too deep for words. ~ Rom. 8:26 ESV

13. I speak in unknown tongues and I pray that I may interpret. I will pray in the spirit and I will pray with an understanding also. ~1 Cor. 14:13, 15a

14. I pray without ceasing. ~1 Thess. 5:17

15. When I am afflicted, I will pray. When I am merry, I will sing psalms. ~James 5:13

16. I, therefore, confess my sins to each other (*meaning to those who are of the household of faith*) and I pray for others, so that I may be healed. The prayer of a righteous person is powerful and effective. ~James 5:16 NIV (Note: Italics are my addition.)

17. First of all, I make supplications, prayers, intercessions, and giving of thanks for all men; for kings, and for all that are in authority, that I/we may lead a quiet and peaceable life in all godliness and honesty. For this is good and acceptable in the sight of God our Savior who would have all men to be saved and to come unto the knowledge of truth. ~1 Tim. 2:1-4

18. I will not be anxious or worry about anything, but in everything [every circumstance and situation] by prayer and petition with thanksgiving, I will continue to make my [specific] requests known to God. And the peace of God [that peace which reassures the heart, that peace], which transcends all understanding, [that peace which] stands guard over my heart and my mind in Christ Jesus [is mine]. ~Phil. 4:6-7 AMP

19. Our Father which art in heaven, Hallowed be thy name. Thy kingdom come, Thy will be done, in earth as it is in heaven. Give us this day our daily bread. And forgive us our debts, as we also forgive our debtors. And lead us not into temptation, but deliver us from evil: For thine is the kingdom, and the power, and the glory, forever. Amen ~Matt. 6:9-13

20. Oh Lord, bless me indeed and enlarge my boarder, and let your hand be with me. Keep me from harm so that it might not bring me pain! ~1 Chron. 4:10 ESV

YOUR POSITION IN CHRIST

1. In Christ Jesus, I am freely justified by His grace through His redemption. ~Rom. 3:24

2. In Christ Jesus, I have no condemnation because I live and walk according to the dictates of the Spirit and not according to the dictates of the flesh. ~Rom. 8:1

3. In Christ Jesus, the law of the Spirit of life has made me free from the law of sin and death. ~Rom. 8:2

4. In Christ Jesus, I have wisdom from God and righteousness, sanctification, and redemption. ~1 Cor. 1:30

5. Now thanks be to God, who always leads me in triumph in Christ and through me diffuses the fragrance of His knowledge in every place. ~2 Cor. 2:14 NKJV

6. In Christ, the veil that was over my heart and mind that stopped me from understanding the Word of God has been removed. ~2 Cor. 3:14-16 ESV

7. In Christ, I am a new creation (*a creature that has never been created before*). Old things have passed away and all things have become new (*the fresh and the new has come*). ~2 Cor. 5:17 (Note: Italics are my addition.)

8. In Christ, I am reconciled to God who does not count my trespasses against me and who entrusts to me (*along with all Christians*) the message of reconciliation. ~2 Cor. 5:19 ESV (Note: Italics are my addition.)

9. In Christ Jesus, I have liberty. ~Gal. 2:4

10. In Jesus Christ, by faith, I have been given the promise of life and righteousness because I believe. Gal. 3:21-22

11. In Christ, I have been blessed with every spiritual blessing in heavenly places by my God and Father of my Lord Jesus Christ. ~Eph. 1:3

12. In Christ, I am God's workmanship, created for good works, which God planned beforehand and prepared ahead of time that I should walk in them. ~Eph. 2:10

13. In Christ, I am raised up together with and made to sit together with Him in heavenly places. ~Eph. 2:6

14. Now in Christ, I who was once excluded from the citizenship in Israel and a foreigner to the covenant of promise and without God in the world have been made near by the blood of Christ. ~Eph. 2:12-13 NIV

15. In Christ Jesus, I give thanks in everything for this is the will of God concerning me. ~1 Thess. 5:18

16. In Christ, I live, move, and have my being. ~Acts 17:28

17. I believe in Christ; therefore, I do not perish, but have eternal life. ~John 3:15

18. In Christ, I have become the righteousness of God because God made Jesus who knew no sin to become sin for me. ~2 Cor. 5:12

19. In Christ, all the promises of God are Yes and Amen to the

glory of God by me/us. ~2 Cor. 1:20

20. In Christ, I am saved and called with a holy calling, not according to my works, but according to His purpose and grace, which was given to me before the world began. ~2 Tim. 1:9

21. In Christ, I am sanctified and called to be a saint with all who in every place call upon the name of Jesus Christ my/ours Lord. ~1 Cor. 1:2

22. In Christ, I know the Holy Scriptures, which are able to make me wise for salvation through faith. ~2 Tim. 3:15

23. I am complete in Christ who is the head of all principality and power. ~Col. 2:10

24. In Christ, I am strong in the power of His might. ~Eph. 6:10

25. I abide in Christ. Therefore, I walk just as He walked. ~1 John 2:6

26. I know that I am in Christ because I keep His word and the love of God is perfected in me. ~1 John 2:5

27. In Christ, there is no sin. ~1 John 3:5

28. In Christ, I have redemption through His blood, the forgiveness of sins according to the riches of His grace. ~Eph. 1:7

29. In Christ, I have obtained an inheritance, being predestined according to the purpose of him who works all things after the counsel of His own will. ~Eph. 1:11

30. In Christ, I reign in life. ~Rom. 5:17b

31. In Christ, I have redemption through His blood, the forgiveness of sins. ~Col. 1:14

32. In Christ, God has reconciled me to Himself and has given me the ministry of reconciliation. ~2 Cor. 5:18

33. In Christ, God supplies all my needs according to His riches in glory. ~Phil. 4:19

34. In Christ, I am enriched in everything, in all speech and all knowledge. ~1 Cor. 1:5 ESV

35. In Christ, I am reconciled to Him for He has made peace (*between Himself and mankind)* through the blood of Christ. ~Col. 1:20 (Note: Italics are my addition.)

36. Through the blood of Christ, my conscience is purified from dead works to serve the living God. ~Heb. 9:14 ESV

37. In Christ, whatever I do in word or deed, I do all in the Name of the Lord Jesus, giving thanks to God the Father through Him. ~Col. 3:17

38. In Christ, I have confidence to enter the holy places by His blood, by the new and living way that He opened for me through the curtain, that is, through His flesh. ~Heb. 10:19-20 ESV

39. In Christ, I am no longer a slave, but I am a son/*daughter* of God and if a son/*daughter*, then an heir of through God. ~Gal. 4:7 ESV (Note: Italics are my addition.)

40. In Christ, I bear much fruit for He is the Vine and I am the branch in Him. I abide in Him and He abides in me for without Him I can do nothing. ~John 15:4-5

41. In Christ, who is the propitiation [the atoning sacrifice that holds back the wrath of God that would otherwise be directed at us because of our sinful nature – our worldliness, our lifestyle]; not for my/our sins alone, but also for [the sins of all believers throughout] the whole world, I have forgiveness for my sins. ~1 John 2:2 AMP

42. In Christ, I abide in Him and He abides in me for I keep His commandments. ~1 John 3:24

43. In Christ, I am complete in Him who is the head of every principality and power. ~Col 2:10

44. In Christ, I have boldness and access with confidence through faith. ~Eph. 3:12

45. In Christ, I have all the treasures of wisdom and knowledge because they are hidden in Him. ~Col. 2:3

46. In Christ, I also am a living stone that is being built up as a spiritual house, to be a holy priesthood, to offer up spiritual sacrifices acceptable to God through Jesus Christ. ~1 Pet. 2:5 ESV

47. In Christ, I can do all things through Him who strengthens me. ~Phil. 4:13

48. In Christ, I can do all things [which He has called me to do] through Him who strengthens and empowers me [to fulfill His purpose – I am self-sufficient in Christ's sufficiency; I am ready for anything and equal to anything through Him who infuses me with inner strength and confident peace]. ~Phil. 4:13 AMP

49. In Christ, I have died with Him and I do now believe that I also live with Him. ~Rom. 6:8

50. In Christ, I have reckoned myself to be dead indeed to sin, but I am alive to God in Christ Jesus our Lord. ~Rom. 6:11 NKJV

FAMILY

1. My family and all the families of the earth are blessed through Abraham. ~Gen. 12:3

2. The Lord is the God of my family and we are His people. ~Jer. 31:1

3. My family, along with all the families in heaven and earth, is of the Father (*meaning of God the Father*). ~Eph. 3:14-15 (Note: Italics are my addition.)

4. Because God commanded the first man and woman to be fruitful and multiply, my family is fruitful and we multiply. ~Gen. 2:27-28

5. I choose this day to serve God. And as for me and my house, we will serve the Lord. ~Josh. 24:15

6. Every good thing and every promise that the Lord swore to my fathers shall come to pass for my family. None of His words to bless and prosper the patriarchy and the matriarchy in my family shall fail. ~Josh. 21:44-45

7. The Lord is the shepherd of my family. Therefore, we shall not want. ~Ps. 23:1

8. The Lord saves me and my family with an everlasting salvation. ~Isa. 47:7a

9. My family is planted in the house of the Lord and we shall flourish in the courts of the Lord. ~Ps. 92:13

10. The Lord builds my house; therefore, my labor is not in vain. ~Ps. 127:1

11. My family and my house bless the Lord. ~Ps. 135:19-20

12. The members of my family do not go at it alone. God sets the lonely in families, He leads out the prisoners with singing. ~Ps. 686a NIV

13. God raises the needy out of affliction. My family is set on high from affliction and the Lord makes my families like flocks. ~Ps. 107:41 ESV & KJV

14. I walk in the blessing of Jubilee. Therefore, my possessions and my family are returned to me. I walk in liberty. Therefore, I am debt free. ~Lev. 25:10

15. God saves my family and me from our enemies and He puts those to shame that hate us. ~Ps. 44:7

16. Because I believe in the Lord Jesus Christ, I am saved, along with everyone in my household. ~Acts 16:31 NLT

17. In my family, God will turn the hearts of the fathers to their children and the hearts of the children to their fathers. Therefore, my family is saved from utter destruction. ~Mal. 4:6 ESV

HUSBAND/FATHER

1. As a husband, I leave my mother and my father and I cleave unto my wife and we are one flesh. ~Gen. 2:24

2. I teach (*the ways of God*) diligently unto my children, and I talk of them when I sit in my house, and when I walk by the way, and when I lay down, and when I rise up. ~Deut. 6:7 (Note: Italics are my addition.)

3. As arrows in the hand of a warrior, so are the children of my youth. I am a blessed man because I have my quiver full of them. I shall not be put to shame when I speak with the enemies in the gate. ~Ps. 127:4-5 ESV

4. My wife shall be as a fruitful vine by the sides of my house: my children like olive plants round about my table. ~Ps. 128:3

5. I find (*or have found*) a wife; therefore, I find (*or have found*) a good thing and I obtain favor of the Lord. ~Prov. 18:22 (Note: Italics are my addition.)

6. I enjoy life with the wife whom I love, all the days of my vain life that the Lord has given me under the sun, because that is my portion in life and in my toil at which I toil under the sun. ~Eccles. 9:9 ESV

7. I leave my father and mother and hold fast to my wife, and what were two shall become one flesh. My wife and I are no longer two but one flesh. What God has joined together, let not man separate. ~Matt. 19:5-6 ESV

8. As a husband, I render due benevolence to my wife and she does likewise. ~1 Cor. 7:3

9. I avoid fornication. I have my own wife. ~1 Cor. 7:2

10. I do not have power over my own body, but my wife does. Therefore, I freely give my body to her. ~1 Cor. 7:4

11. I am the head of my wife, even as Christ is the head of the church: and He is the savior of the Body. ~Eph. 5:23

12. I love my wife as Christ loved the church and gave Himself for her. Therefore, I give myself for my wife and I consider her before I consider myself. ~Eph. 5:25 ESV

13. As a father, I do not provoke my children to wrath, but I bring them up in the nurture and admonition of the Lord. ~Eph. 6:4

14. As a husband, I love my wife and I am not bitter against her. ~Col. 3:19

15. As a father, I do not provoke my children to anger. ~Col. 3:21

16. As a husband, I dwell with my wife in an understanding way, showing honor to her, the woman, as the weaker vessel, since she is an heir with me of the grace of life, so that my prayers may not be hindered. ~1 Pet. 3:7 ESV

17. I submit to my wife and she submits to me in the fear of the Lord. ~Eph. 5:21

18. My wife is subject to me. ~1 Pet. 3:5

19. My fountain is blessed and I rejoice in the wife of my youth, as a lovely deer, and graceful doe. I let her breast fill me at all times with delight; and I am intoxicated always in her love. ~Prov. 5:18-19

20. I have a prudent wife from the Lord. ~Prov. 19:14

21. I love my wife as I love my own body. I love my wife; thereby, loving myself. ~Eph. 5:28

22. My children keep the commandments of their father and do not forsake the teaching of their mother. ~Prov. 6:20

23. My children are wise and I rejoice in them. ~Prov. 23:25

WIFE/MOTHER

1. As a wife, I shall be as a fruitful vine by the sides of my husband's house. Our children shall be like olive plants round about his table. ~Ps. 128:3

2. My husband leaves his mother and his father and he cleaves to me and we are one flesh. ~Gen. 2:24

3. I teach (*the ways of God*) diligently to my children, and I talk of them when I sit in my house, and when I walk by the way, and when I lay down, and when I rise up. ~Deut. 6:7 (Note: Italics are my addition.)

4. My husband finds (*or has found*) me, his wife; therefore, he finds (*or has found*) a good thing and he obtains (*or has obtained*) the favor of the Lord. ~Prov. 18:22 (Note: Italics are my addition.)

5. My husband leaves his father and mother and hold fast to me, and what were two shall become one flesh. My husband and I are no longer two but one flesh. What God has joined together, let not man separate. ~Matt. 19:5-6 ESV

6. I avoid fornication. I have my own husband. ~1 Cor. 7:2

7. I do not have power over my own body, but my husband

does. Therefore, I freely give my body to him. ~1 Cor. 7:4

8. As a wife, I submit to my own husband, as unto the Lord. ~Eph. 5:22

9. My husband and I submit ourselves to one another in the fear of God. ~Eph. 5:22

10. My husband is my head, even as Christ is the head of the church: and He is the savior of the Body. ~Eph. 5:23

11. My husband loves me as Christ loved the church and gave Himself for her. ~Eph. 5:24

12. I am subject to my own husband in everything, just as the church is subject to Christ. ~Eph. 5:24

13. Just as Christ sanctifies and cleanses the church with the washing of the water by the word, my husband sanctifies and cleanses me by his words. ~Eph. 5:26

14. My husband loves me as he loves his own body. ~Eph. 5:28

15. I am reverent in behavior, not a slanderer or slave to much wine. I teach the young women what is good, and I train them to love their husbands and children, to be self-controlled, pure, working at home, kind, submissive to their own husbands, that the word of God may not be reviled. ~Titus 2:4-5 ESV

16. I am a prudent wife from the Lord. ~Prov. 19:14

17. As a believing wife, I sanctify my unbelieving husband. Whereas, our children were unclean, they are now holy. ~1 Cor. 7:14

18. As a wife, I care for the things of the world, how I may please my husband. ~1 Cor. 7:34b

19. My husband gives me honor as the weaker vessel and his prayers are unhindered. ~1 Pet. 3:7

20. My husband rejoices in me, the wife of his youth. My breasts fill him with delight at all times. He is intoxicated always in my love. ~Prov. 5:18-19 ESV

21. I am a wife of noble character (*a virtuous woman*). I am worth far more than rubies. My husband has confidence in me and lacks nothing of value. I bring him good, not harm, all the days of his life. ~Prov. 31:10-12 NIV (Note: Italics are my addition.)

22. All around town, I am known as a virtuous woman. As virtuous woman, I am a crown to my husband. ~Ruth 3:11; Prov. 12:4

23. I am a joyful mother of children. My children rise up and call me blessed, my husband also and he praises me. ~Ps. 113:9; Prov. 31:28

24. I am a wise woman and I build my house. ~Prov. 14:1

CHILDREN

As a parent meditating on and/or confessing these scriptures, where it says, "I," you may want to say, "my children" or "my child" and vice versa. You may also call your child or children by name. Moreover, you can teach your children to meditate on, make these confessions, and pray over themselves.

1. I honor my father and mother, as the Lord my God commanded me and my days are long and it is well with me in the land which the Lord my God gives me. ~Deut. 5:16

2. I hear the instructions of my father and do not forsake the law of my mother; for they are graceful ornaments on my head and chains about my neck. ~Prov. 1:8-9

3. I remember the law of my father and my heart keeps his commandments. For they add length of days, long life, and peace to me. ~Prov. 3:1-2

4. I hear the instructions of my father and pay close attention in order to gain and to know intelligent discernment, comprehension, and interpretation [of spiritual matters]. ~Prov. 4:1 AMP

5. I attend to God's wisdom and bow my ear to His understanding that I may regard discretion and that my lips may keep knowledge. ~Prov. 5:1-2

6. I keep God's words and I treasure up his commandments with me. I keep his commandments and live; keep his teaching as the apple of my eye. I bind them on my finger. I write them on the tablet of my heart. I say to wisdom, "You are my sister," and I call insight my intimate friend, to keep me from the forbidden woman, from the adulteress with her smooth words ~Prov. 7:1-5 ESV

7. I am a wise son/daughter; therefore, I make my father glad. ~Prov. 15:20

8. I am trained up in the way that I should go in the Lord: and when I am old, I will not depart from it. ~Prov. 22:6

9. I obey my parents in the Lord for it is right and it is well with me, and I live long on the earth. ~Eph. 6:1, 3

10. I am brought up in the training and admonition of the Lord. ~Eph. 6:4

11. I listen to my father who gave me life and do not despise my mother when she is old. ~Prov. 23:22

12. I obey my parents in all things: for this is well pleasing to the Lord. ~Col. 2:20

13. I seek to know the Holy Scriptures from childhood that I may grow wise in my faith in Christ Jesus. ~2 Tim. 3:15

14. I do not let anyone despise my youth, but I am an example to the believers in word, in conduct, in love, in spirit, in faith, and in purity. ~1 Tim. 4:12

15. My parents make known the parables and dark sayings of God to me. They make known to me the things that they

have heard and known, the things that their fathers have told them. They do not hide them from their children, but they tell to the coming generation the glorious deeds of the Lord, and his might, and the wonders that He has done. ~Ps. 75:2-4

16. Children are a heritage from the Lord and the fruit of the womb is His reward. Therefore, as my parent's child, I am a heritage and His reward to them. ~Ps. 127:3

17. I rise up and call my mother blessed. ~Prov. 31:28

18. I am taught of the Lord and great shall be my peace. ~Isa. 54:13

19. The Spirit of the Lord is upon my parents and He has put His words in their mouths. His words shall not depart out of their mouths, or out of the mouths of their offspring, or out of the mouths of their children's offspring. ~Isa. 59:21 ESV

20. I am the offspring of the righteous; therefore, I will be delivered. ~Prov. 11:21b ESV

THE CHURCH/BODY OF CHRIST

1. On this rock (*the revelation of who Christ is*), Christ will build his church; and the gates of hell shall not prevail against His church. ~Matt. 16:18 ESV (Note: Italics are my addition.)

2. The Lord adds to the church daily those who should be saved. ~Acts 2:47

3. Now you/we are the body of Christ and individually members of it. And God has appointed in the church first apostles, second prophets, third teachers, then miracles, then gifts of healings, helping, administrating, and various kinds of tongues. ~1 Cor. 12:27-28 ESV

4. He who speaks in an unknown tongue edifies himself, but he who prophesies edifies the church. ~1 Cor. 14:4

5. As much as I am/we are zealous of spiritual gifts, I/we seek that I/we may excel to the edifying of the church. ~1 Cor. 14:12

6. God has put all things under Christ's feet and gave him to be the head over all things to the church, which is his body, the fullness of him that fills all in all. ~Eph. 1:22-23

7. The church makes known the manifold wisdom of God to the principalities and powers in heavenly places. According to the eternal purpose which God purposed in Christ Jesus our Lord: in whom we have boldness and access with confidence by the faith of him…. For this cause, I bow my knees unto the Father of our Lord Jesus Christ, of whom the whole family in heaven and earth is named, that he would grant you, the church, according to the riches of his glory, to be strengthened with might by his Spirit in the inner man; that Christ may dwell in your hearts by faith; that we, being rooted and grounded in love, may be able to comprehend what is the breadth, and length, and depth, and height and to know the love of Christ, which passes knowledge, that we might be filled with all the fullness of God. ~Eph. 3:10-12, 14-19

8. God receives glory in the church by Christ Jesus throughout all ages, world without end. Amen. ~Eph. 3:21

9. Christ is the head of the church. ~Eph. 5:23; Col. 1:18

10. Christ loved the church and gave Himself for it; that he might sanctify and cleanse it with the washing of water by the word, that he might present it to himself a glorious church, not having spot, or wrinkle, or any such thing; but that it should be holy and without blemish. ~Eph. 5:25-27

11. The Lord nourishes and cherishes the church. ~Eph. 5:29

12. The people of God know how they should behave themselves in the house of God, which is the church of the living God, the pillar and ground of truth. ~1 Tim. 3:15

13. I/We also have died to the law through the body of Christ, so that I/we may belong to another, to him who has been raised from the dead, in order that I/we may bear fruit for God. ~Rom. 7:4 ESV

14. I walk worthy of the vocation of which I was called, with all

lowliness and meekness, with longsuffering, forbearing one another in love; endeavoring to keep the unity of the Spirit in the bond of peace. There is only one body and one Spirit, even as we are called in one hope of our calling; One Lord, one faith, one baptism, and one God and Father of all, who is above all, through all and in all. But unto every believer is given grace according to the measure of the gift of Christ. ~Eph. 4:1-7

15. Christ gave the apostles, the prophets, the evangelist, the shepherds (*pastors*), and teachers; to equip the saints for the work of the ministry, for building up the body of Christ, until we all attain to the unity of the faith and of the knowledge of the Son of God, to mature manhood, to the measure of the stature of the fullness of Christ, so that we may no longer be children, tossed to and fro by the waves and carried about by every wind of doctrine, by human cunning, by craftiness in deceitful schemes. Rather speaking the truth in love, we are to grow up in every way into him, who is the head, into Christ, from whom the whole body, joined together by every joint with which it is equipped, when each part is working properly, makes the body grow so that it builds itself up in love. ~Eph. 4:11-16 ESV (Note: Italics are my addition.)

16. There is one body and one Spirit, even as you are called in one hope of your calling; one Lord, one faith, one baptism, one God and Father of all, who is above all, and through all, and in you all. ~Eph. 4:4-6

17. In accordance to what Christ prayed to God the Father, I am one with every believer in Christ. As the Father is in Christ and Christ is in the Father, we (*the believers*) are also made one in them; that the whole world may believe that the Father sent the Son. And that the glory, which the Father gave the Son, has been given to us (*the believers*); that we may be one, even as the Father and the Son are one. Christ is in us and the Father in the Son, so that we may be made perfect in one; and that the world may know that the Father has sent the Son and has loved us (*the believers*), as He

loved the Son. Because the Father has given us (*the believers*) to the Son, we behold the glory of the Son, which the Father gave Him before the foundation of the world. The world has not known the Father, but Jesus Christ, the Son, has known the Father, and his disciples have known that the Father sent him. The Son has declared the Father's name and will declare the Father's name: that the love that the Father loved the Son with may be in us (*the believers*) and Christ in us (*the believers*). ~John 17:21-24, 26 (Note: Italics are my addition.)

18. I, along with every believer, am sanctified through God's truth: His word is truth. ~John 17:17

THE COMMUNITY

1. May God Almighty bless <u>(Name your community)</u> and make you fruitful and increase your numbers until you become a community of peoples. ~Gen. 28:3 NIV

2. God will make <u>(Name your community)</u> a community of peoples, and He will give the land he promised you as an everlasting possession to your descendants after you. ~Gen. 48:4 NIV

3. May the LORD, the God of the spirits of all mankind, appoint a man over <u>(Name your community)</u> to go out and come in before them, one who will lead them out and bring them in, so the LORD's people will not be like sheep without a shepherd. ~Num. 27:16-17 NIV

19. God will restore the fortunes of Jacob's (*His people's*) tents and have compassion on his dwellings; the city will be rebuilt on her ruins, and the palace will stand in its proper place. From them will come songs of thanksgiving and the sound of rejoicing. God will add to their numbers, and they will not be decreased; God will bring them honor, and they will not be disdained. Their children will be as in days of old, and their community will be established before Him. He will punish all who oppress them. Their leader will be one of their own. Their ruler will arise from among them. God will

bring him near and he will come close to Him, for who is he who will devote himself to be close to Me? says the LORD. So you will be my people, and I will be your God. ~Jer. 30:18-22 (Note: Italics are my addition.)

4. The Lord is returned unto our <u>(Name your city)</u> and He will dwell in the midst of our city: and ours shall be called a city of truth; and the mountain of the LORD of hosts the holy mountain. There shall yet old men and old women dwell in the <u>(Name your city)</u>, and every man with his staff in his hand for a multitude of days. And the streets of the city shall be full of boys and girls playing in the streets thereof. ~Zech. 8:3-5

5. God rids me and delivers me from the hand of strange children, whose mouth speaks vanity, and their right hand is a right hand of falsehood: that our sons may be as plants grown up in their youth; that our daughters may be as corner stones, polished after the similitude of a palace: that our garners may be full, according all manner of store: that our sheep may bring forth thousands and ten thousands in our streets: that our oxen may be strong to labor; that there be no breaking in, nor going out; that there be no complaining in our streets. Happy is that people, that is in such a case: yea, happy is that people, whose God is the LORD. ~Ps. 144:11-15

6. Our city, along with its foundations, places of worship and walls are being rebuilt. And our enemies are financing it, just like in the days of Ezra and Nehemiah. ~Ezra 4-6; Neh. 2 *(Read and study the books of Ezra and Nehemiah, so that God can prepare your heart for what He wants to restore and rebuild in your city. Let God give you a heart for His city and a strategy, then let Him empower you to be the man or woman of God who will do the work and make a difference in your community/city.)*

7. There is a river, the streams whereof shall make glad the city of God, the holy place of the tabernacles of the most High.

God is in the midst of her; she shall not be moved: God shall help her and that right early. God is in the midst of our city. Our city is the city of God and God helps her and that right early. ~Ps. 46:4-5

8. The Lord keeps our city; the watchman does not wake in vain. ~Ps. 127:1

9. When it goes well with the righteous, (Name your city) rejoices: and when the wicked perish, there is shouting. By the blessing of the upright (Name your city) is exalted. ~Prov. 11:10-11

THE GOVERNMENT

1. (Name your government) is upon the shoulders of Christ Jesus and his name shall be called Wonderful, Counselor, The Mighty God, The Everlasting Father, The Prince of Peace. There shall be no end of the increase of his government and peace. ~Is. 9:6-7

2. Christ was given authority, glory, and sovereign power; all peoples, nations, and men of every language worship him. His dominion is an everlasting dominion that will not pass away, and his kingdom is one that will never be destroyed. ~Dan. 7:14 NIV

3. Christ has given me/us authority to trample on snakes and scorpions and to overcome all the power of the enemy; nothing will harm me/us. ~Luke 10:19-20

20. First of all, I/we make supplication, prayers, intercessions, and giving of thanks for all men; for kings (name them) (*This is where you would name presidents, governmental leaders, etc.*), and for all that are in authority (name them) (*This is where you would name presidents, governmental leaders, etc.*); that I/we may lead a quiet and peaceable life in all godliness and honesty. For this is good and acceptable in the sight of God my/our Savior; who will have all men to be saved, and to come unto the knowledge of the truth.

~1 Tim. 2:1-4 (Note: Italics are my addition.)

4. I/We submit myself/ourselves to the governing authorities, for there is no authority except that which God has established. The authorities that exist have been established by God. ~Rom. 13:1

5. Christ is the highest authority. God has given Christ all power. He is the head over every power and authority. Therefore, he is the highest authority over all the governments of the heavens, earth, and beneath. ~Eph. 1:19-23; Col. 2:10 NIV

6. At the name of Jesus, every knee shall bow and every tongue shall confess that Jesus Christ is Lord. ~Phil 2:10

7. Our (Name your nation) is blessed because our God is the LORD. Our people are blessed because He has chosen us for His own inheritance. ~Ps. 33:12

8. Righteousness exalts our nation. ~Prov. 14:34

9. For God loves (Name your nation), and He has built us a place for His habitation, a house of worship. ~Luke 7:5

10. We are a chosen generation, a royal priesthood, a holy nation, a peculiar people; that we should show forth the praises of him who has called us out of darkness into his marvelous light. ~1 Pet. 2:9

BLESSINGS AND PROSPERITY

1. I am a faithful man; therefore, I abide in blessings. ~Prov. 28:20

2. I am a tither; therefore, God opens the windows of heaven and pours out blessings upon me that I do not have room enough to receive it. ~Mal. 3:10

3. I listen diligently to the voice of the Lord my God, being watchful to do all His commandments, which He commands me. The Lord sets me on high above all the nations of the earth. And all these blessings shall come upon me and overtake me. I am blessed in the city and blessed in the field. Blessed shall be the fruit of my body and the fruit of my ground and the fruit of my beasts, the increase of my cattle and the young of my flock. Blessed shall be my basket and my kneading trough. Blessed shall I be when I come in and blessed shall I be when I go out. The Lord shall cause my enemies who rise up against me to be defeated before my face. They shall come out against me one way and flee before me seven ways. The Lord shall command the blessing upon me in my storehouse and in all that I undertake. And He will bless me in the land, which He gives me. The Lord will establish me as a people holy to Him, as He has sworn to me, if I keep the commandments of the Lord my God and walk in His ways. All the people of the earth shall see that I

am called by the name (and in the presence of) the Lord, and they shall be afraid of me. The Lord shall make me have a surplus of prosperity, through the fruit of my body, of my livestock, and of my ground, in the land, which he swore to my fathers to give me. The Lord shall open to me His good treasury, the heavens, to give the rain to my land in its season and to bless all the work of my hands; and I shall lend to many nations, but I shall not borrow. The Lord shall make me the head, and not the tail; and I shall be above only, and I shall not be beneath, if I heed the commandments of the Lord my God. ~Deut. 28:1-13 AMP

4. The Lord is with me and He makes me successful and prosperous. The Lord makes all that I do to flourish and succeed in my hand. ~Gen. 39:3-4

5. I delight myself in the Lord and He gives me the desires of my heart. ~Ps. 37:4

6. This is the day that the Lord has made. I will rejoice and be glad in it. The Lord saves me and sends me prosperity ~Ps. 118:24-25

7. The Lord is my Shepherd and I shall not want. ~Ps. 23:1

8. God's Word does not depart out of my mouth, but I meditate in it day and night that I may observe to do according to all that is written in it. For then I will make my way prosperous and I will have good success. ~Josh. 1:8

9. I seek first the kingdom of God and His righteousness and all these things are added unto me. ~Matt. 6:33

10. In all my labor there is profit. ~Prov. 14:23a

11. I am wise in the Lord and He crowns me with riches. ~Prov. 14:24

12. I sow bountifully and I reap bountifully. I give cheerfully

and not grudgingly or of necessity, and God loves me and makes all grace abound towards me, that I always having all sufficiency in all things, have an abundance for every good work. ~2 Cor. 9:6-8

13. God supplies all my needs according to His riches in glory by Christ Jesus. ~Phil. 4:19

14. It is the will of God that I prosper in all things and be in good health, even as my soul prospers. ~3 John 2

15. Christ has redeemed me from the curse of poverty, sickness, and death. I now have the blessings of Abraham. ~Gal. 3:13

16. Jesus Christ became poor for my sake, so that through His poverty, I might become rich. ~2 Cor. 8:9

17. I fear the Lord and I have no want. The young lions do lack and suffer hunger, but I seek the Lord and I shall not lack any good thing. ~Ps. 34:9, 10

18. I fear the Lord and delight greatly in His commandments; therefore, wealth and riches are in my house. ~Ps. 112:1, 3

19. By humility and the fear of the Lord, I receive riches, honor, and life. ~Prov. 22:4

20. My delight is in the law of the Lord and in His law I do meditate day and night. I am like a tree planted by the rivers of water that brings forth its fruit in its season, whose leaf also shall not wither. Whatever I do shall prosper. ~Ps. 1:2-3

21. I am the righteousness of God by one Christ Jesus; therefore, the Lord does not allow my soul to famish. I am diligent and He makes me rich. ~Rom. 3:22; Rom. 10:3; Prov. 10:3-4

22. I am willing and obedient and I eat the good of the land. ~Is. 1:19

23. I give and it will be given back to me; good measure, pressed down, and shaken together, and running over, shall men give into my bosom. For with the same measure that I mete withal it shall be measured to me again. ~Luke 6:38

24. I bless the Lord for He daily loads me with benefits, even the God of our salvation. ~Ps. 68:19

25. My soul blesses the Lord and does not forget His benefits who forgives all my iniquities, who heals all my diseases; who redeems my life from destruction; who crowns me with lovingkindness and tender mercies; who satisfies my mouth with good things; so that my youth is renewed like the eagle's. ~Ps. 103:3-5

26. The commandments of the Lord prolong my life and bring me prosperity. ~Pr. 3:1-2

27. I pursue righteousness and love and I find life, prosperity, and honor. ~Prov. 21:21 NIV

28. I am blessed because I fear the LORD and walk in His ways. Therefore, I will eat the fruit of my labor; blessings and prosperity will be mine. ~Ps. 128:1-2 NIV

29. I am the righteousness of God by one Christ Jesus; therefore, prosperity is my reward. ~Prov. 13:21 NIV

30. I dwell in the secret place of the Most High; therefore, I shall abide under the shadow of the Almighty. I will say of the Lord, He is my refuge and my fortress: My God, in Him will I trust. Surely He shall deliver me from the snare of the fowler and from the noisome pestilence. He shall cover me with His feathers and under His wings shall I trust. His truth shall be my shield and buckler. I shall not be afraid for the terror by night; nor for the arrow that flies by day; nor for the pestilence that walks in darkness nor for the destruction that wastes at noonday. A thousand shall fall by my side and ten thousand at my right hand, but it shall not come near me.

Only with my eyes shall I behold and see the reward of the wicked. Because I have made the Lord, which is my refuge, even the Most High, my habitation, there shall no evil befall me, neither shall any plague come near my dwelling. For the Lord shall give His angels charge over me, to keep me in all my ways. His angels shall bear me up in their hands, lest I dash my foot against a stone. I shall tread upon the lion and adder: the young lion and dragon shall I trample under feet. Because I have set my love upon the Lord; therefore, He will deliver me. He will set me on high because I have known His name. I shall call upon the Lord and He will answer me. He will be with me in trouble. He will deliver me and honor me. With long life, He will satisfy me and show me His salvation. ~Ps. 91

PRAYER JOURNAL

Keep a journal of your prayer activities.

PRAYER JOURNAL

Date Prayed: **Date Answered:**

Prayer Topic:

Prayer:

Scripture: (Confession/Meditations, etc.)

Insights/Revelations:

PRAYER JOURNAL

Date Prayed: **Date Answered:**

Prayer Topic:

Prayer:

Scripture: (Confession/Meditations, etc.)

Insights/Revelations:

PRAYER JOURNAL

Date Prayed: **Date Answered:**

Prayer Topic:

Prayer:

Scripture: (Confession/Meditations, etc.)

Insights/Revelations:

PRAYER JOURNAL

Date Prayed: **Date Answered:**

Prayer Topic:

Prayer:

Scripture: (Confession/Meditations, etc.)

Insights/Revelations:

PRAYER JOURNAL

Date Prayed: **Date Answered:**

Prayer Topic:

Prayer:

Scripture: (Confession/Meditations, etc.)

Insights/Revelations:

PRAYER JOURNAL

Date Prayed: **Date Answered:**

Prayer Topic:

Prayer:

Scripture: (Confession/Meditations, etc.)

Insights/Revelations:

PRAYER JOURNAL

Date Prayed: **Date Answered:**

Prayer Topic:

Prayer:

Scripture: (Confession/Meditations, etc.)

Insights/Revelations:

PRAYER JOURNAL

Date Prayed: **Date Answered:**

Prayer Topic:

Prayer:

Scripture: (Confession/Meditations, etc.)

Insights/Revelations:

PRAYER JOURNAL

Date Prayed: **Date Answered:**

Prayer Topic:

Prayer:

Scripture: (Confession/Meditations, etc.)

Insights/Revelations:

PRAYER JOURNAL

Date Prayed: **Date Answered:**

Prayer Topic:

Prayer:

Scripture: (Confession/Meditations, etc.)

Insights/Revelations:

PRAYER JOURNAL

Date Prayed: **Date Answered:**

Prayer Topic:

Prayer:

Scripture: (Confession/Meditations, etc.)

Insights/Revelations:

PRAYER JOURNAL

Date Prayed: **Date Answered:**

Prayer Topic:

Prayer:

Scripture: (Confession/Meditations, etc.)

Insights/Revelations:

PRAYER JOURNAL

Date Prayed: **Date Answered:**

Prayer Topic:

Prayer:

Scripture: (Confession/Meditations, etc.)

Insights/Revelations:

PRAYER JOURNAL

Date Prayed: **Date Answered:**

Prayer Topic:

Prayer:

Scripture: (Confession/Meditations, etc.)

Insights/Revelations:

PRAYER JOURNAL

Date Prayed: **Date Answered:**

Prayer Topic:

Prayer:

Scripture: (Confession/Meditations, etc.)

Insights/Revelations:

PRAYER JOURNAL

Date Prayed: **Date Answered:**

Prayer Topic:

Prayer:

Scripture: (Confession/Meditations, etc.)

Insights/Revelations:

PRAYER JOURNAL

Date Prayed: **Date Answered:**

Prayer Topic:

Prayer:

Scripture: (Confession/Meditations, etc.)

Insights/Revelations:

PRAYER JOURNAL

Date Prayed: **Date Answered:**

Prayer Topic:

Prayer:

Scripture: (Confession/Meditations, etc.)

Insights/Revelations:

PRAYER JOURNAL

Date Prayed: **Date Answered:**

Prayer Topic:

Prayer:

Scripture: (Confession/Meditations, etc.)

Insights/Revelations:

PRAYER JOURNAL

Date Prayed: **Date Answered:**

Prayer Topic:

Prayer:

Scripture: (Confession/Meditations, etc.)

Insights/Revelations:

PRAYER JOURNAL

Date Prayed: **Date Answered:**

Prayer Topic:

Prayer:

Scripture: (Confession/Meditations, etc.)

Insights/Revelations:

PRAYER JOURNAL

Date Prayed: **Date Answered:**

Prayer Topic:

Prayer:

Scripture: (Confession/Meditations, etc.)

Insights/Revelations:

PRAYER JOURNAL

Date Prayed: **Date Answered:**

Prayer Topic:

Prayer:

Scripture: (Confession/Meditations, etc.)

Insights/Revelations:

PRAYER JOURNAL

Date Prayed: **Date Answered:**

Prayer Topic:

Prayer:

Scripture: (Confession/Meditations, etc.)

Insights/Revelations:

PRAYER JOURNAL

Date Prayed: **Date Answered:**

Prayer Topic:

Prayer:

Scripture: (Confession/Meditations, etc.)

Insights/Revelations:

PRAYER JOURNAL

Date Prayed: **Date Answered:**

Prayer Topic:

Prayer:

Scripture: (Confession/Meditations, etc.)

Insights/Revelations:

PRAYER JOURNAL

Date Prayed: **Date Answered:**

Prayer Topic:

Prayer:

Scripture: (Confession/Meditations, etc.)

Insights/Revelations:

PRAYER JOURNAL

Date Prayed: **Date Answered:**

Prayer Topic:

Prayer:

Scripture: (Confession/Meditations, etc.)

Insights/Revelations:

PRAYER JOURNAL

Date Prayed: **Date Answered:**

Prayer Topic:

Prayer:

Scripture: (Confession/Meditations, etc.)

Insights/Revelations:

PRAYER JOURNAL

Date Prayed: **Date Answered:**

Prayer Topic:

Prayer:

Scripture: (Confession/Meditations, etc.)

Insights/Revelations:

PRAYER JOURNAL

Date Prayed: **Date Answered:**

Prayer Topic:

Prayer:

Scripture: (Confession/Meditations, etc.)

Insights/Revelations:

PRAYER JOURNAL

Date Prayed: **Date Answered:**

Prayer Topic:

Prayer:

Scripture: (Confession/Meditations, etc.)

Insights/Revelations:

PRAYER JOURNAL

Date Prayed: **Date Answered:**

Prayer Topic:

Prayer:

Scripture: (Confession/Meditations, etc.)

Insights/Revelations:

PRAYER JOURNAL

Date Prayed: **Date Answered:**

Prayer Topic:

Prayer:

Scripture: (Confession/Meditations, etc.)

Insights/Revelations:

PRAYER JOURNAL

Date Prayed: **Date Answered:**

Prayer Topic:

Prayer:

Scripture: (Confession/Meditations, etc.)

Insights/Revelations:

CHART YOUR WALK

*Track your steps/miles and prayer activities
as you exercise your body and exercise your faith.*

CHART YOUR WALK

Date	Step/Miles	Prayer Topic

CHART YOUR WALK

Date	Step/Miles	Prayer Topic

CHART YOUR WALK

Date	Step/Miles	Prayer Topic

CHART YOUR WALK

Date	Step/Miles	Prayer Topic
Date	Step/Miles	Prayer Topic

CHART YOUR WALK

Date	Step/Miles	Prayer Topic
Date	Step/Miles	Prayer Topic

CHART YOUR WALK

Date	Step/Miles	Prayer Topic

CHART YOUR WALK

Date	Step/Miles	Prayer Topic

CHART YOUR WALK

Date	Step/Miles	Prayer Topic

CHART YOUR WALK

Date	Step/Miles	Prayer Topic
Date	Step/Miles	Prayer Topic

CHART YOUR WALK

Date	Step/Miles	Prayer Topic
Date	Step/Miles	Prayer Topic

CHART YOUR WALK

Date	Step/Miles	Prayer Topic

CHART YOUR WALK

Date	Step/Miles	Prayer Topic

CHART YOUR WALK

Date	Step/Miles	Prayer Topic

CHART YOUR WALK

Date	Step/Miles	Prayer Topic

CHART YOUR WALK

Date	Step/Miles	Prayer Topic

CHART YOUR WALK

Date	Step/Miles	Prayer Topic

CHART YOUR WALK

Date	Step/Miles	Prayer Topic

CHART YOUR WALK

Date	Step/Miles	Prayer Topic

CHART YOUR WALK

Date	Step/Miles	Prayer Topic

CHART YOUR WALK

Date	Step/Miles	Prayer Topic

CHART YOUR WALK

Date	Step/Miles	Prayer Topic

NOTES

Write your thoughts, curiosities, ideas, inspirations, etc.

NOTES

NOTES

NOTES

NOTES

NOTES

GET STARTED: EXPAND YOUR WORLD IMPACT

If you would like to receive the Walk & Pray Strategy, learn more about how you can get involved, and/or charter a Walk & Pray group or team at your church, in your community, or with your organization, please contact us. Moreover, if you would really like to make major impact, contact us about organizing a Walk & Pray Transform-a-thon.

<u>Contact us:</u>

Lisa B. Taylor
Email: drlisabtaylor@gmail.com
Website: www.lisabtaylor.com